W9-BTH-733

SIDE BY SIDE

FOOTBALL STARS

Comparing Pro Football's Greatest Players

BY SHANE FREDERICK

CAPSTONE PRESS
a capstone imprint

SIDE-BY-SIDE FOOTBALL STARS:
Comparing Pro Football's Greatest Players

The National Football League (NFL) is full of great individual matchups. Quarterbacks Tom Brady and Peyton Manning have faced each other three times in the AFC playoffs as they tried to reach the Super Bowl. Denver Broncos legend John Elway faced both the 49ers' Joe Montana and the Packers' Brett Favre in Super Bowls. The Cowboys and the Bills played each other in back-to-back Super Bowls after the 1992 and 1993 seasons. The teams had two of the best running backs in the league in Dallas' Emmitt Smith and Buffalo's Thurman Thomas.

But what if the best players of today could take on the best players of the past? Would Adrian Peterson outshine Walter Payton? Would J.J. Watt be more dominant than Reggie White? Could you imagine a Super Bowl between Joe Montana and Tom Brady? Let's put those players side by side and see who stands out!

*All stats are through the 2013 season.

Sports Illustrated Kids Side-By-Side Sports are published by Capstone Press,
1710 Roe Crest Drive, North Mankato, Minnesota 56003
www.capstonepub.com

Sports Illustrated Kids is a trademark of Time Inc. Used with permission.

Printed in the United States of America in Stevens Point, Wisconsin.
032014   008092WZF14

TABLE OF CONTENTS

ADRIAN PETERSON

NICKNAME: All Day
HEIGHT: 6 feet, 2 inches (188 cm)
WEIGHT: 217 pounds (98 kg)
YEARS ACTIVE: 2007–present*
TEAM: Vikings
PRO BOWLS: 6
FIRST-TEAM ALL-PRO: 3
MVP AWARDS: 1
2007 ROOKIE OF THE YEAR
2008 PLAYER OF THE YEAR
-Led NFL in rushing yards twice

Games	Rushing Yards	Yards/Carry	Yards/Game	Rushing TDs
103	10,115	5.0	98.2	86

*Stats are through the 2013 season.

WALTER
PAYTON

NICKNAME: Sweetness
HEIGHT: 5 feet, 10 inches (178 cm)
WEIGHT: 200 pounds (91 kg)
YEARS ACTIVE: 1975–1987
TEAM: Bears
PRO BOWLS: 9
FIRST-TEAM ALL-PRO: 5
SUPER BOWL CHAMPIONSHIPS: 1
MVP AWARDS: 1
1985 PLAYER OF THE YEAR
-Led NFL in rushing yards once
-Ranks second all-time in rushing yards
-Entered the Hall of Fame in 1993

Games	Rushing Yards	Yards/Carry	Yards/Game	Rushing TDs
190	16,726	4.4	88.0	110

"I say if there is a human superhero, it's Adrian Peterson." —*Philadelphia Eagles tight end Brett Celek*

"I want to be the best player to ever play this game." —*Adrian Peterson*

Adrian Peterson burst onto the NFL scene as a first-year player. He rushed for 296 yards in a single game in 2007—an all-time single-game record—and was named Rookie of the Year. A season later he led the league in rushing and looked unstoppable. Late

in the 2011 season, however, Peterson suffered a devastating knee injury, tearing his anterior cruciate ligament (ACL). People wondered if he'd ever be the same, and if so, how long it would take to get there.

Less than nine months later, Peterson was back in a Vikings uniform, ready to give it a try. But he wasn't the same—he was better. In 2012 Peterson put together one of the best seasons by a running back in NFL history. He rushed for 2,097 yards—nine yards short of breaking Eric Dickerson's single-season record. He wasn't afraid of hurting his knee again either. More than half of his yardage that season came after a defender hit him.

WALTER PAYTON

Former Bears coach Mike Ditka called Walter Payton the best football player who ever lived. Not just the best running back, but the best football player. On a cold, windy November day in 1977 at Chicago's Soldier Field, Payton certainly proved it. Despite having a case of the flu, Payton rushed for 275 yards—a single-game record that stood for 23 seasons. He also had a touchdown in the Bears' 10-7 win over the Minnesota Vikings. Payton was practically a one-man team that day. He carried the ball 40 times, while the Bears only completed four of seven passes, including one to Payton. "Sweetness" won the MVP that season, averaging 132.3 yards rushing per game—the third-best average in NFL history. Seven years later, he passed the great Jim Brown as the NFL's all-time leading rusher and held the record until 2002.

"He was a warrior, the best-conditioned, strongest guy pound-for-pound, a great runner, great blocker, receiver, great all-around. And the biggest thing he had was his great will and heart, and that's what drove him."

—*Former Chicago Bears coach Mike Ditka*

"Give me the heart of Walter Payton. There's never been a greater heart."

—*Hall of Fame running back Jim Brown*

PEYTON MANNING

NICKNAME: The Sheriff
HEIGHT: 6 feet, 5 inches (196 cm)
WEIGHT: 230 pounds (104 kg)
YEARS ACTIVE: 1998–present*
TEAM: Colts, Broncos
PRO BOWLS: 13
FIRST-TEAM ALL-PRO: 7
SUPER BOWL CHAMPIONSHIPS: 1
MVP AWARDS: 5
PLAYER OF THE YEAR AWARDS: 2
2012 COMEBACK PLAYER OF THE YEAR

-Led NFL in passing yards three times and
    TD passes four times
-Ranks second all-time in completions,
    passing yards, and passing touchdowns

Games	Completions-Attempts	Yards	Yards/Game	TDs	Interceptions
240	5,532-8,452 (65.5%)	64,964	270.7	491	219

*Stats are through the 2013 season.

DAN MARINO

NICKNAME: Dan the Man
HEIGHT: 6 feet, 4 inches (193 cm)
WEIGHT: 224 pounds (102 kg)
YEARS ACTIVE: 1983–1999
TEAM: Dolphins
PRO BOWLS: 9
FIRST-TEAM ALL-PRO: 3
MVP AWARDS: 1
PLAYER OF THE YEAR AWARDS: 1
1994 COMEBACK PLAYER OF THE YEAR

-Led NFL in passing yards five times and
   TD passes three times
-Ranks third all-time in passing yards
   and passing touchdowns
-Entered the Hall of Fame in 2005

Games	Completions-Attempts	Yards	Yards/Game	TDs	Interceptions
242	4,967-8,358 (59.4%)	61,361	253.6	420	252

PEYTON MANNING

In May of 2011, Peyton Manning had surgery on his neck. The recovery and rehabilitation caused him to miss all of the following season. Some people thought it might end his career. He was 35 years old and had spent 13 seasons with the Indianapolis Colts. Had he retired, Manning would have gone down as one of the all-time greats. He was a Super Bowl champion, winning the big game's MVP in 2006, and the NFL's only four-time MVP. He was second all-time behind Brett Favre in career completions, passing yards, and touchdown passes.

After his year off, Manning joined the Denver Broncos, and fans soon realized he wasn't even close to being done. He led Denver to a 13-3 record, throwing for 4,659 yards and 37 touchdowns. The next season, he led the Broncos back to the Super Bowl, tossing a record 55 touchdown passes along the way.

"He's the best that's ever played this game as far as quarterbacks are concerned. When he's retired, they'll compare everybody to Peyton Manning, without a doubt."
—*Former teammate and NFL wide receiver Brandon Stokley*

"He's probably the hardest-working guy I've been around who has great ability. Overachievers work hard because they have to. Peyton has rare talent, but chooses to push himself like he doesn't." —*Former Indianapolis Colts coach Tony Dungy*

DAN MARINO

When Dan Marino entered the NFL in 1983, the league was still years away from featuring the high-flying passing game that it has today. Had he come around two or three decades later, who knows what kind of numbers he would have put up? What he was doing at the time had never been done before.

In 1984, his second season with the Miami Dolphins, Marino smashed NFL passing records. He became the first

quarterback to surpass the 5,000-yard mark in a single season, and his 48 touchdown passes were 12 more than the previous record. Marino retired in 1999, holding 19 passing records and sharing five others. His 420 career touchdown passes were 78 more than the old record. Although players from the passing era have since taken over those records, Marino set the modern-day standard.

"You were basically at Dan's mercy. All the great ones see the game so quickly that when everybody else is running around like a chicken with his head cut off, they know exactly where they want to go with the ball. It's like they see everything in slow motion."

—*Hall of Fame defensive back Ronnie Lott*

"I always had the feeling that with Dan at quarterback, we were never out of the game, no matter what the score."

—*Former Miami Dolphins coach Don Shula*

CALVIN JOHNSON

NICKNAME: Megatron
HEIGHT: 6 feet, 5 inches (196 cm)
WEIGHT: 239 pounds (108 kg)
YEARS ACTIVE: 2007–present*
TEAM: Lions
PRO BOWLS: 4
FIRST-TEAM ALL-PRO: 3
-Led NFL in receptions once, TD catches once,
   and receiving yards twice
-Holds single-season receiving yards record

Games	Receptions	Yards	Yards/Game	Receiving TDs
106	572	9,328	88.0	66

*Stats are through the 2013 season.

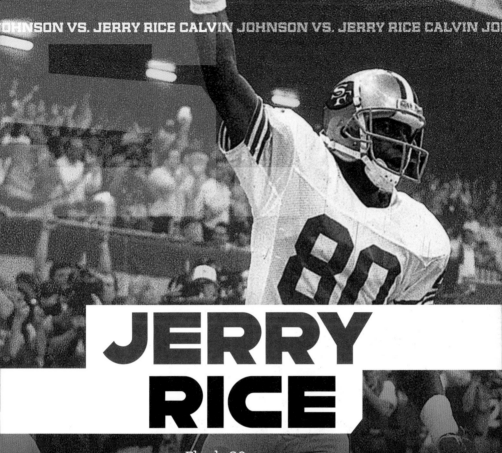

JERRY RICE

NICKNAME: Flash 80
HEIGHT: 6 feet, 2 inches (188 cm)
WEIGHT: 200 pounds (91 kg)
YEARS ACTIVE: 1985–2004
TEAMS: 49ers, Raiders, Seahawks
PRO BOWLS: 13
FIRST-TEAM ALL-PRO: 10
SUPER BOWL CHAMPIONSHIPS: 3
MVP AWARDS: 1

-*Led NFL in receptions twice, TD catches six times, and receiving yards six times*
-*All-time leader in receiving TDs, overall TDs, receptions, and receiving yards*
-*Entered the Hall of Fame in 2010*

Games	Receptions	Yards	Yards/Game	Receiving TDs
303	1,549	22,895	75.6	197

CALVIN JOHNSON

There's a reason Calvin Johnson is nicknamed "Megatron." The Detroit Lions wide receiver doesn't seem human. The towering receiver becomes a pass-catching machine when the ball is in the air. Running a deep post route with two defensive backs trying to stay stride for stride with him, Johnson suddenly leaps into the air. He appears to keep rising even as the defenders start dropping back to the turf. He grabs the ball and regains his balance as he brushes off a cornerback and safety like crumbs before jogging into the end zone. It's just another "freak-show catch," according to his quarterback, Matthew Stafford.

Megatron continues to show why he's at the top of the receiving class. In 2012 Johnson set the single-season mark for receiving yards with 1,964. The next year he broke a 14-year-old receiving record by racking up 329 yards in a single game.

> "I love having him as a teammate. I love throwing the ball to him. He goes through a lot. He gets hit. He's getting the ball a bunch and he's taking a beating out there. ... He just sets a great standard for all the guys on our team and really everybody in this league."
>
> —Teammate and Detroit Lions quarterback Matthew Stafford

> "It is unbelievable. He is one of the best players I have ever seen, if not the best. The skill set and just the ability that he has is head and shoulders above anyone that I have ever seen."
>
> —Teammate and Detroit Lions receiver Kris Durham

14

JERRY RICE

"He can catch a BB on a dead run at night."

—*Archie Cooley, Rice's coach at Mississippi Valley State University*

"I've never seen a player more driven or willing to work harder to become the greatest of all time. His perfectionism was evident in everything he did, in the way he carried himself both on and off the field." —*Edward DeBartolo Jr., former owner of the San Francisco 49ers*

When Jerry Rice began playing professional football, the NFL record for career touchdown receptions was 99. Four years into Rice's career, the Seahawks' Steve Largent, playing in his final NFL season, broke that record by one. By the time Rice retired, he not only had the record, but he may have put it too far out of reach for anyone to catch. The number to beat now is 197 receiving touchdowns!

Rice played 20 seasons in the NFL and helped the San Francisco 49ers win three Super Bowls. In Super Bowl XXIII, he had 11 catches for 215 yards and was named MVP. Rice, who had 11 straight 1,000-yard receiving seasons, also ran for 10 touchdowns and recovered a fumble for a score. He finished his career with 208 total touchdowns—33 more than the next player on the list.

J.J. WATT

NICKNAME: J.J. Swat
HEIGHT: 6 feet, 5 inches (196 cm)
WEIGHT: 290 pounds (132 kg)
YEARS ACTIVE: 2011–present*
TEAM: Texans
PRO BOWLS: 2
FIRST-TEAM ALL-PRO: 2
2012 DEFENSIVE PLAYER OF THE YEAR
-Led NFL in sacks once

Games	Sacks	Tackles	Assists	Turnovers
48	36.5	192	37	6

*Stats are through the 2013 season.

REGGIE
WHITE

NICKNAME: The Minister of Defense
HEIGHT: 6 feet, 5 inches (196 cm)
WEIGHT: 291 pounds (132 kg)
YEARS ACTIVE: 1985–2000
TEAMS: Eagles, Packers, Panthers
PRO BOWLS: 13
FIRST-TEAM ALL-PRO: 8
1987 AND 1998 DEFENSIVE PLAYER OF THE YEAR
-Led NFL in sacks twice
-Ranks second all-time in sacks
-Entered the Hall of Fame in 2006

Games	Sacks	Tackles	Assists	Turnovers
232	198.0	1,048	63	23

In 2012 no player was feared more in the NFL than the Houston Texans' J.J. Watt. Opposing quarterbacks had to make sure they knew where Watt was before every snap, and even then there wasn't much that could be done to stop him. By the end of the season, Watt had put together one of the finest seasons ever by a defensive player. Watt led the NFL with 20.5 sacks and 81 tackles, including 23 tackles for a loss of yards.

One of Watt's most amazing statistics that season was his 16 passes defended—a stat normally reserved for cornerbacks and safeties. Watt was the top non-defensive back in that category, thanks to his ability to knock down and tip passes at the line of scrimmage. That skill earned him the nickname "J.J. Swat."

"I'm at a loss for words for that guy. It never gets old. You see him make plays week after week and you wonder at what point he is going to slow down. But it's not happening."

—Houston Texans offensive lineman Duane Brown

"I think he's a defensive lineman that does everything well. He really has no weaknesses. ... All he has are strengths."

—NFL defensive lineman Richard Seymour

REGGIE WHITE

The NFL's free agency rules changed in 1993, and no player was more sought after than Reggie White. The longtime pass rusher with double-digit sack totals in each of his eight seasons with the Philadelphia Eagles was free to sign with another team. The two-time Defensive Player  of the Year opted to join the Green Bay Packers, a team from the smallest city in the NFL. The Packers had been down on their luck for more than two decades. White transformed the team back into a winner and champion.

Perhaps White's best game as a Packer came in Super Bowl XXXI. Using a variety of power rushing moves to blow by blockers, he made life miserable for the Patriots' Drew Bledsoe that day. His three quarterback sacks in that game still stands as a Super Bowl record nearly two decades later.

"He may have been [the] best player I've ever seen and certainly was the best I've ever played with or against."

—Former teammate and NFL quarterback Brett Favre

"On the football field, White was a rare combination of size, power and speed. He was one of those guys who stepped up and made special plays when his team needed him to come through. Like all great players, he had a great sense of knowing when to seize the moment." —Former quarterback Joe Theismann

TOM BRADY

NICKNAME: Tom Terrific
HEIGHT: 6 feet, 4 inches (193 cm)
WEIGHT: 225 pounds (102 kg)
YEARS ACTIVE: 2000–present*
TEAM: Patriots
PRO BOWLS: 9
FIRST-TEAM ALL-PRO: 2
SUPER BOWL CHAMPIONSHIPS: 3
MVP AWARDS: 2
2007 OFFENSIVE PLAYER OF THE YEAR
2009 COMEBACK PLAYER OF THE YEAR
TWO-TIME SUPER BOWL MVP
-Led NFL in TD passes three times and passing yards twice
-Ranks fifth all-time in TD passes

Games	Completions-Attempts	Yards	Yards/Game	TDs	Interceptions
193	4,178-6,586 (63.4%)	49,149	254.7	359	134

*Stats are through the 2013 season.

JOE
MONTANA

NICKNAME: Joe Cool
HEIGHT: 6 feet, 2 inches (188 cm)
WEIGHT: 200 pounds (91 kg)
YEARS ACTIVE: 1979–1994
TEAMS: 49ers, Chiefs
PRO BOWLS: 8
FIRST-TEAM ALL-PRO: 3
MVP AWARDS: 2
1986 COMEBACK PLAYER OF THE YEAR
1989 OFFENSIVE PLAYER OF THE YEAR
SUPER BOWL CHAMPIONSHIPS: 4
THREE-TIME SUPER BOWL MVP
-Ranks 11th all-time in TD passes
-Entered the Hall of Fame in 2002

Games	Completions-Attempts	Yards	Yards/Game	TDs	Interceptions
192	3,409-5,391 (63.2%)	40,551	211.2	273	139

"Tom Brady is just the greatest. He's just so hard to play against."
—*Former Dallas Cowboys coach Wade Phillips*

"Who would you rather have running your two-minute drill? I'll take Tom Brady 10 out of 10 times." —*Former Patriots offensive coordinator Charlie Weis*

In the second game of the 2001 season, New England Patriots starting quarterback Drew Bledsoe went down with an injury. In came a little-known second-year player who had been drafted the previous year in the sixth round. At the time, no one knew that NFL history was being made. Bledsoe's backup, Tom Brady, quickly became a star. He led the Patriots to their first Super Bowl championship that year, starting a dynasty in New England.

With Brady at quarterback, the Patriots have been to five Super Bowls, winning three titles. In 2007 Brady led the Pats to an undefeated regular season and the highest-scoring total in NFL history at the time. New England averaged 36.8 points per game that year, and Brady broke the single-season record for touchdown passes with 50.

JOE MONTANA

The San Francisco 49ers trailed the Cincinnati Bengals by three points with 3 minutes, 20 seconds remaining in Super Bowl XXIII. They were 92 yards away from the end zone. Cool and calm, quarterback Joe Montana gathered his nervous teammates and looked up into the crowd. There he spotted a famous actor, John Candy, and pointed him out to the guys in the huddle. If Joe wasn't worried, the other players thought, why should they be? With renewed confidence, the team marched down the field. Montana completed eight passes, including a 10-yard touchdown pass to John Taylor for the winning score with 34 seconds left. It was Montana's third Super Bowl win. A year later, he got his fourth championship, tossing five touchdown passes and no interceptions against the Denver Broncos. He passed for 800 yards and 11 scores in the 1989 postseason alone.

"There have been, and will be, much better arms and legs and much better bodies on quarterbacks in the NFL, but if you have to win a game or score a touchdown or win a championship, the only guy to get is Joe Montana." —*Former teammate and 49ers offensive lineman Randy Cross*

"Joe was born to be a quarterback. ... How many guys are there who can do what he can do? Him, maybe [Dan] Marino on a good day. Perhaps God had a hand in this thing."

—*Montana's high school quarterback coach, Jeff Petrucci*

AARON
RODGERS

NICKNAME: Mr. Rodgers
HEIGHT: 6 feet, 2 inches (188 cm)
WEIGHT: 223 pounds (101 kg)
YEARS ACTIVE: 2005–present*
TEAM: Packers
PRO BOWLS: 3
FIRST-TEAM ALL-PRO: 1
SUPER BOWL CHAMPIONSHIPS: 1
MVP AWARDS: 1
2010 SUPER BOWL MVP
-Led NFL in passer rating twice
-All-time leader in passer rating

Games	Completions-Attempts	Yards	Yards/Game	TDs	Interceptions
94	1,945-2,955 (65.8%)	24,197	257.4	188	52

*Stats are through the 2013 season.

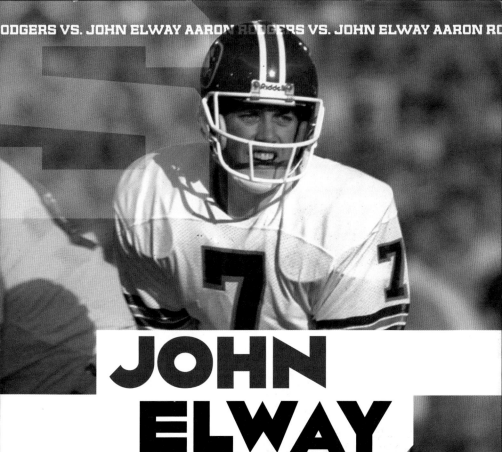

JOHN ELWAY

NICKNAME: The Comeback Kid
HEIGHT: 6 feet, 3 inches (191 cm)
WEIGHT: 215 pounds (98 kg)
YEARS ACTIVE: 1983–1998
TEAM: Broncos
PRO BOWLS: 9
SUPER BOWL CHAMPIONSHIPS: 2
MVP AWARDS: 1
1998 SUPER BOWL MVP
-Led NFL in passing yards once
-Ranks fourth all-time in passing yards and
 seventh in TD passes
-Entered the Hall of Fame in 2004

Games	Completions-Attempts	Yards	Yards/Game	TDs	Interceptions
234	4,123-7,250 (56.9%)	51,475	220.0	300	226

AARON RODGERS

For nearly 16 full seasons, the Packers didn't have to worry about the quarterback position. Brett Favre never missed a start in his time in Green Bay. When the Packers elevated Aaron Rodgers to starter and traded Favre to the New York Jets in 2008, it seemed like a big risk. But Rodgers continued the tradition of great quarterback play in Green Bay, joining Favre and the legendary Bart Starr.

Rodgers even accomplished something Favre didn't, winning the Super Bowl MVP award. In Super Bowl XLV, Rodgers was 24 for 39, passing for 304 yards and three touchdowns as the Packers beat the Pittsburgh Steelers. A year later, Rodgers was named the NFL's MVP as he led the Packers to a 15-1 record during the regular season.

"I can't even begin to tell you how sharp he is and how well he retains things. He is a student of the game. He loves it. He submerges himself in it. He doesn't just memorize things. He understands concepts."

—Jeff Tedford, Rodgers' coach at the University of California, Berkeley

"He's been great since the first time he stepped on the field, but I think the one thing is he's more and more consistent. You add that to his talent and you see what you get."

—Former NFL quarterback Kurt Warner

JOHN ELWAY

John Elway led Denver to the Super Bowl three times in the 1980s, and the Broncos lost all of them. In the 1986 AFC championship against the Cleveland Browns, he led his team on a touchdown drive over the game's final 5 minutes to force overtime. Starting at his own 2-yard line, Elway passed for 78 yards and scrambled for 20. "The Drive," as it is now known, defined Elway's career.

A decade later, in Super Bowl XXXII, Elway led the Broncos down the field 92 yards for a touchdown that gave his team a third-quarter lead. The key play was a scramble for a first down. The 37-year-old Elway was hit by three defenders on the run, and he spun in the air like the blades of a helicopter. The Broncos upset the Green Bay Packers for their first championship that game. A year later, Elway led Denver to a second title.

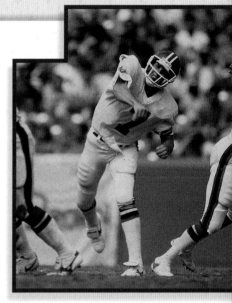

"John Elway is the master of the inconceivable pass thrown to the unreachable spot."

—*Broadcaster and former NFL player Pat Summerall*

"John Elway may be one of the best all-time quarterbacks, particularly in the clutch. When the game was on the line, he was like Michael Jordan—he wanted the football. In those situations, I don't know if I know anyone that did a better job of handling that than John did."

—*Former Denver Broncos coach Dan Reeves*

ARIAN FOSTER

HEIGHT: 6 feet (183 cm)
WEIGHT: 232 pounds (105 kg)
YEARS ACTIVE: 2009–present*
TEAM: Texans
PRO BOWLS: 3
FIRST-TEAM ALL-PRO: 1
-Led NFL in rushing yards once, rushing TDs twice, and rushing/receiving TDs twice

Games	Rushing Yards	Yards/Carry	Yards/Game	Rushing TDs
59	5,063	4.5	85.8	45

EMMITT SMITH

HEIGHT: 5 feet, 9 inches (175 cm)
WEIGHT: 202 pounds (92 kg)
YEARS ACTIVE: 1990–2004
TEAMS: Cowboys, Cardinals
PRO BOWLS: 8
FIRST-TEAM ALL-PRO: 4
SUPER BOWL CHAMPIONSHIPS: 3
MVP AWARDS: 1
1990 OFFENSIVE ROOKIE OF THE YEAR
-*All-time leader in rushing yards and rushing TDs*
-*Ranks second all-time in total touchdowns*
-*Entered the Hall of Fame in 2010*

Games	Rushing Yards	Yards/Carry	Yards/Game	Rushing TDs
226	18,355	4.2	81.2	164

ARIAN FOSTER

As a college player at the University of Tennessee, Arian Foster ran the ball for nearly 3,000 yards, becoming that program's all-time leading rusher. But when his college career was over, every NFL team passed on him in the draft. He eventually signed with the Houston Texans and spent most of 2009, his first professional season, as a practice player. The next spring, the Texans selected a running back in the second round, but Foster grabbed the job once the season started. In the first game, Foster carried the ball 33 times for 231 yards and three touchdowns against the Indianapolis Colts. By the end of the season, he topped the league in rushing yards. Only two running backs in NFL history reached 5,000 yards from scrimmage faster than Foster, who reached that milestone in just 40 games.

"I understand that it's rare in this league to go undrafted and perform at the level that I did. What people don't understand is that it didn't just happen. I worked day and night at my craft."
—*Arian Foster*

"The first thing is that Arian's a three-down player. It's hard to find guys these days who never leave the field. A lot of guys play first [and] second down. Then you have third-down backs that can catch a ball better, do those type of things. ... Arian is just a very well-rounded player."
—*Former Houston Texans coach Gary Kubiak*

EMMITT SMITH

The average length of an NFL running back's career is less than three years. Emmitt Smith played the taxing position for 15 years. He racked up more than 1,000 yards in 11 straight seasons on his way to becoming the league's all-time leading rusher.

The Dallas Cowboys' superstar wasn't afraid of playing hurt. He earned the reputation of being one of the toughest running backs in history. At the end of the 1993 season, Smith suffered a separated shoulder during an important game against the New York Giants. The painful injury should have sent him to the bench. But he stayed in the game, running for 168 yards and making 10 catches for 61 yards and a touchdown. Four weeks later, Smith was named Super Bowl MVP as the Cowboys won their second straight championship.

"He'll take your breath away, and you won't get it back until he scores."

—*Former Dallas Cowboys running backs coach Joe Brodsky*

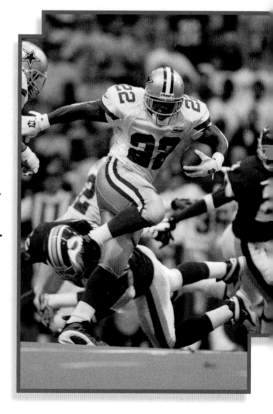

"No question, he has the biggest heart here. He expects to win games and he doesn't expect anyone else to do it for him. Because he cares."

—*Former teammate and Cowboys safety Darren Woodson*

LARRY
FITZGERALD

NICKNAME: Fitz
HEIGHT: 6 feet, 3 inches (191 cm)
WEIGHT: 225 pounds (102 kg)
YEARS ACTIVE: 2004–present*
TEAM: Cardinals
PRO BOWLS: 8
FIRST-TEAM ALL-PRO: 1
-Led NFL in receptions once and receiving TDs twice

Games	Receptions	Yards	Yards/Game	Receiving TDs
156	846	11,367	72.9	87

*Stats are through the 2013 season.

CRIS
CARTER

NICKNAME: C.C.
HEIGHT: 6 feet, 3 inches (191 cm)
WEIGHT: 202 pounds (92 kg)
YEARS ACTIVE: 1987–2002
TEAMS: Eagles, Vikings, Dolphins
PRO BOWLS: 8
FIRST-TEAM ALL-PRO: 2

-Led NFL in receptions once and receiving
  TDs three times
-Ranks fourth all-time in receptions and
  receiving TDs
-Entered the Hall of Fame in 2013

Games	Receptions	Yards	Yards/Game	Receiving TDs
234	1,101	13,899	59.4	130

LARRY FITZGERALD

For years the Arizona Cardinals were better known for losing than winning. Before 2008 they had been to the playoffs just twice in a span of 32 years. But with a player like Larry Fitzgerald Jr., the sky's the limit for any team.

In Arizona's run to Super Bowl XLII, Fitzgerald was nothing short of dominant. Opposing teams simply couldn't stop him. In three playoff games that year, he caught 23 passes for 419 yards and four touchdowns. In the Super Bowl against the Pittsburgh Steelers, Fitzgerald finished with seven catches for 127 yards and two touchdowns. With his size, speed, strength, and hands, Fitzgerald has the ability to leap higher than cornerbacks, sprint past safeties, and wrestle the ball away from double and triple coverage.

"He doesn't look like the fastest player, but he kind of gallops and gains ground. He's got long speed, he can out-physical you on short routes, and he can jump over guys."

—NFL cornerback Nnamdi Asomugha

"I'm taking the same approach Jerry Rice took. He was a 10-time All-Pro, and that never meant anything to him. Guys are going to be prepared for me every week. I'm going to have to get myself in the best condition I've ever been in."

—Larry Fitzgerald

CRIS CARTER

In 1990 the Philadelphia Eagles decided they didn't want Cris Carter on their team anymore. He was a good player, but not good enough over his three seasons there. "All he does is catch touchdown passes," Philadelphia coach Buddy Ryan said. The Minnesota Vikings picked up Carter and quickly discovered he could do much more than that.

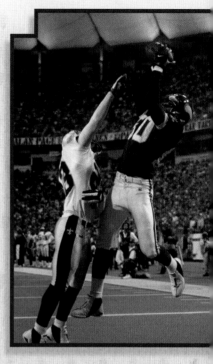

His best moments with the Vikings didn't necessarily take place in the end zone, but rather near the sideline. Carter had a unique ability to reach out and catch a ball while keeping the tips of his toes in bounds. With Minnesota, he caught more than 120 passes in consecutive seasons and became just the second wide receiver to make 1,000 career catches. By the end of his 16-year career, Carter was among the NFL's all-time leaders in catches, yards, and touchdowns.

"Defending Cris is extremely difficult. You never want to cover him inside your 20-yard line because he has such great leaping ability. The only thing you can do is play the ball and hope you can get it before he does."

—Former teammate and NFL defensive back Eric Allen

"It doesn't seem to bother him to have defenders around. He can jump through the roof, and he has stretching ability. He can make both his arms and hands long."

—Former Minnesota Vikings assistant coach Jerry Rhome

JOE
THOMAS

HEIGHT: 6 feet, 7 inches (201 cm)
WEIGHT: 311 pounds (141 kg)
YEARS ACTIVE: 2007–present*
TEAM: Browns
PRO BOWLS: 7
FIRST-TEAM ALL-PRO: 4
GAMES STARTED: 112

*Stats are through the 2013 season.

ANTHONY MUÑOZ

HEIGHT: 6 feet, 6 inches (198 cm)
WEIGHT: 278 pounds (126 kg)
YEARS ACTIVE: 1980–1992
TEAM: Bengals
PRO BOWLS: 11
FIRST-TEAM ALL-PRO: 9
GAMES STARTED: 184
-*Entered the Hall of Fame in 1998*

JOE THOMAS

When a team drafts an offensive lineman with a high pick, the hope is to get a great player who will hold the job for many years. The Cleveland Browns got that with the University of Wisconsin's Joe Thomas when they made him the third overall pick in 2007. Through seven seasons, the durable Thomas not only started every game for the Browns, but he played every offensive snap—a streak of 6,795 plays. It didn't take long for people to consider him one of the best left tackles in the league. He uses his long arms and quick feet to keep oncoming pass rushers away from his quarterback. Thomas was named to the Pro Bowl in each of his first seven seasons. The only other Cleveland player to accomplish that feat was Hall of Fame running back Jim Brown.

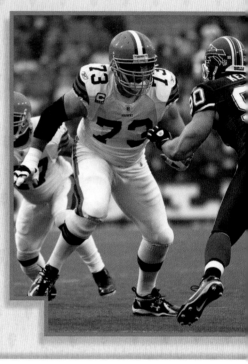

"Sometimes you forget the gravity of how successful and how great some players are. This team has something special in Joe. He's a phenomenal athlete."

—*Teammate and offensive lineman Garrett Gilkey*

"I can't say enough great things about Joe Thomas. ... One hundred games in a row is almost unheard of. It speaks to his durability and how good he is. I'm just glad he's on our team." —*Former Cleveland Browns coach Rob Chudzinski*

ANTHONY MUÑOZ

Who says offensive linemen aren't athletes? Anyone who believes that didn't see Anthony Muñoz play left tackle for the Cincinnati Bengals. Muñoz played both football and baseball at the University of Southern California. He was a good pitcher, but football seemed to suit him best. The Bengals selected him with the third overall pick in the 1980 NFL draft, and they didn't have to worry about that position for 13 years.

Muñoz helped his team win three division titles and a pair of AFC championships to reach two Super Bowls. He started 183 of 185 games over his Hall of Fame career. Besides driving back defensive linemen and shutting down pass rushers, Muñoz got to show off his athleticism by catching seven passes, including four for touchdowns.

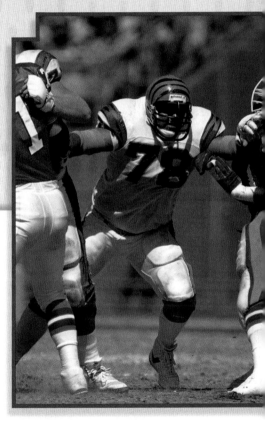

"He's definitely the best athlete on the team. I think he may be the greatest athlete ever to play on the interior line."
—*Former Cincinnati Bengals offensive line coach Jim McNally*

"If I were as good at my position as Anthony is at his, then I'd be 10 times better than Joe Montana."
—*Former teammate and NFL quarterback Boomer Esiason*

RICHARD
SHERMAN

HEIGHT: 6 feet, 3 inches (191 cm)
WEIGHT: 195 pounds (88 kg)
YEARS ACTIVE: 2011–present*
TEAM: Seahawks
PRO BOWLS: 1
FIRST-TEAM ALL-PRO: 2
SUPER BOWL CHAMPIONSHIPS: 1
-Led the NFL in interceptions once and ranked second once

Games	Interceptions	Fumble Recoveries	TDs	Tackles	Assists
48	20	3	2	141	35

*Stats are through the 2013 season.

DEION SANDERS

NICKNAME: Prime Time
HEIGHT: 6 feet, 1 inch (185 cm)
WEIGHT: 195 pounds (88 kg)
YEARS ACTIVE: 1989–2005
TEAMS: Falcons, 49ers, Cowboys, Redskins, Ravens
PRO BOWLS: 8
FIRST-TEAM ALL-PRO: 6
SUPER BOWL CHAMPIONSHIPS: 2
1994 DEFENSIVE PLAYER OF THE YEAR
-Led NFL in non-offensive touchdowns three times
-Tied for first all-time in non-offensive touchdowns
-Entered the Hall of Fame in 2011

Games	Interceptions	Fumble Recoveries	TDs	Tackles	Assists
188	53	13	10	492	20

41

RICHARD SHERMAN

Richard Sherman isn't built like most cornerbacks. He's tall and has a long reach like a wide receiver. In fact, when he was in college at Stanford University, he started off as a receiver before coaches suggested he switch to defense after an injury. Sherman still thinks like a receiver, though. He has a keen sense for when the difficult-to-defend underthrown pass is coming, and has turned those plays into defensive touchdowns. His size, leaping ability, and physical play has allowed him to pick off or knock away the ball before it gets to its intended target.

In his first three seasons, Sherman was credited with defending 61 passes to go along with 20 interceptions. In the NFC championship game after the 2013 season, he tipped away a last-minute pass into the end zone. His incredible play led the Seattle Seahawks to the Super Bowl, where they crushed the Denver Broncos and earned their first championship.

"Even when he's wrong, he's right. When he gets beat, it's just an opportunity to come back and win more battles."

—Teammate and receiver Doug Baldwin

"Look how quickly he has become what he is. That's what's really amazing, just to see that and at that position. That's a hard position, cornerback, playing against these guys in this league." —Former NFL wide receiver Michael Irvin

DEION SANDERS

"He was an amazing player. You always wanted to watch from the sidelines and see what he was doing. You didn't want to miss anything."

—*Former teammate and NFL offensive lineman Flozell Adams*

"Just watching him and his knack for making big plays ... he was a guy that could do it all. ... He definitely inspired a lot of young guys coming out to play cornerback."—*NFL defensive back Charles Woodson*

There comes a point for great NFL cornerbacks when they stop getting opportunities to do their magic. That was often the case for Deion Sanders. In his 14-year career, he had 53 interceptions, including nine that went for touchdowns. Some quarterbacks would simply avoid throwing to a receiver being covered by the man known as "Prime Time" and "Neon Deion."

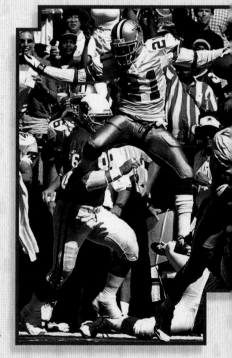

But Sanders could hurt opponents in other ways. He returned six punts and three kickoffs for touchdowns. He also scored touchdowns on three fumble recoveries and three pass receptions as a wide receiver. A standout baseball player as well, Sanders is the only athlete to play in a Super Bowl and a World Series. In 1992 he attempted to become the first athlete to play two pro sports on the same day. He suited up for Atlanta's Falcons and Braves that day but never got in the baseball game.

COACH'S CALL

Adrian Peterson vs. Walter Payton

Both Peterson and Payton have had the ability to carry their teams to victory by themselves. Peterson is an "All Day" back at a time when teams use multiple runners. But Payton's No. 2 ranking on the all-time rushing list gives him a slight advantage. The pick: Payton.

Peyton Manning vs. Dan Marino

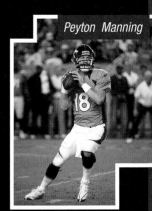

Peyton Manning

Manning and Marino may go down as the greatest passers in NFL history. Marino's stats are impressive, coming from an era before passing dominated the game. Still, Manning eclipsed all of those numbers and won a title. The pick: Manning.

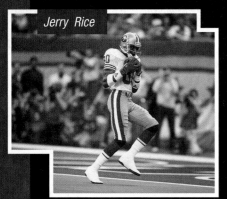

Jerry Rice

Calvin Johnson vs. Jerry Rice

There are times when it seems impossible for teams to defend Johnson. He's simply bigger and stronger and can jump higher than everybody else. Rice, though, holds all of the records. He may be the greatest football player—not just receiver—of all time. The pick: Rice.

J.J. Watt vs. Reggie White

What Watt has done in a short amount of time is impressive. If he keeps it up, he'll join White among the greats. However, White changed the game and changed a franchise. The pick: White.

Tom Brady vs. Joe Montana

This might be the toughest decision in the book. Brady had better seasons than Montana. But no one was better in Super Bowls than Montana. He gets the edge in title games, going 4-0 to Brady's 3-2. The pick: Montana.

Aaron Rodgers vs. John Elway

Elway led the Broncos to five Super Bowls and won two of them before retiring. Rodgers is one of the most efficient quarterbacks to play in the NFL, but he has just one championship so far. The pick: Elway.

Arian Foster vs. Emmitt Smith

Smith is the NFL's all-time rushing king and played for 15 years. Arian Foster had one of the best starts to a career that a running back could have but was slowed by a back injury in 2013. The pick: Smith.

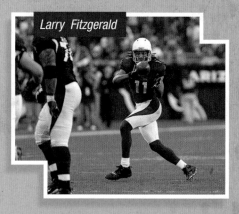

Emmitt Smith

Larry Fitzgerald

Larry Fitzgerald vs. Cris Carter

Fitzgerald learned how to play wide receiver from Carter when he was a ball boy with the Vikings. Both have great hands and great feet. For this coach, the student has surpassed the teacher. The pick: Fitzgerald.

Joe Thomas vs. Anthony Muñoz

Muñoz may go down as the greatest offensive lineman of all time. Joe Thomas could be in the running someday. He is having a great start to his career but hasn't reached that status yet. The pick: Muñoz.

Richard Sherman vs. Deion Sanders

Sherman is one of the best, most-feared cornerbacks in the game today. There's a toughness to him that many DBs don't have. But Deion Sanders also could beat teams by returning kicks and punts. The pick: Sanders.

Critical Thinking Using the Common Core

1. Reread pages 4–7. Who has a better single-season rushing record, Adrian Peterson or Walter Payton? (Key Ideas and Details)

2. Reread pages 12–15 and 32–35. If you had to pick one of the four receivers to be on your team, who would you choose? Why? Support your choice with information from the text. (Key Ideas and Details)

3. Look at the choices the author made on pages 44 and 45 of the Coach's Call section. Do you agree with his picks? Why or why not? Support your choices with information from this title, as well as from other books or online sources. (Integration of Knowledge and Ideas)

Quotation Sources

www.vikings.com, 6a; http://cowboysblog.dallasnews.com, 6b; www.espn.go.com, 7a, 11a, 15a, 19a, 22a, 23a, 23b, 27a; http://nflcommunications.com, 7b; www.jockbio.com, 10a, 10b, 22b, 26a, 30a; www.profootballhof.com, 11b, 27b, 31a, 31b, 35a, 35b, 43a, 43b; www.prideofdetroit.com, 14a; www.detroitlions.com, 14b; www.ninersnation.com, 15b; www.houstontexans.com, 18a, 18b, 30b; Ross, Alan. *I Remember Reggie White.* Nashville: Cumberland House Publishing, Inc., 2005, 19b; www.jsonline.com, 26b; http://sportsillustrated.cnn.com, 34a, 34b, 39b; www.clevelandbrowns.com, 38a, 38b; www.sun-sentinel.com, 39a; www.mercurynews.com, 42a; www.seahawks.com, 42b

Read More

Der, Bob, ed. *Sports Illustrated Kids Big Book of Who Football.* New York: Time Home Entertainment Inc., 2013.

Frederick, Shane. *The Ultimate Collection of Pro Football Records.* Sports Illustrated Kids. North Mankato, Minn.: Capstone Press, 2013.

Hetrick, Hans. *The Super Bowl: All About Pro Football's Biggest Event.* Sports Illustrated Kids. North Mankato, Minn.: Capstone Press, 2013.

Wiseman, Blaine. *Football.* Record Breakers. New York: Weigl, 2011.

Internet Sites

FactHound offers a safe, fun way to find Internet sites related to this book. All of the sites on FactHound have been researched by our staff.

Here's all you do:

Visit *www.facthound.com*

Type in this code: 9781476561653

Check out projects, games and lots more at
www.capstonekids.com

Index

Library of Congress Cataloging-in-Publication Data

Frederick, Shane.
  Side-by-side football stars : comparing pro football's greatest players / by Shane Frederick.
    pages cm.—(Sports Illustrated kids. Side-by-side sports)
  Includes bibliographical references and index.
  Summary: "Compares the greatest pro football players in history"—Provided by publisher.
  ISBN 978-1-4765-6165-3 (library binding)
  ISBN 978-1-4765-6170-7 (paperback)
  1. Football players—United States—Biography—Juvenile literature. 2. Football players—Rating of—Juvenile literature. I. Title.
  GV939.A1F74 2015
  796.3320922—dc23   2014007821

Editorial Credits

Anthony Wacholtz, editor; Ted Williams, designer; Eric Gohl, media researcher; Gene Bentdahl, production specialist

Photo Credits

Getty Images: George Gojkovich, 37, Ron Vesely, 39; Newscom: Cal Sport Media/Chris Szagola, 36, Icon SMI/Kellen Micah, 38, UPI Photo Service/Bob Carey, 41, UPI Photo Service/Ian Halperin, 43, ZUMA Press/Jeff Wheeler, 35; Sports Illustrated: Al Tielemans, 12, 19, 22, 31, Andy Hayt, 7, 17, 23, 27, 44 (bottom), Bill Frakes, 9, 45 (top), Bob Rosato, 24, Damian Strohmeyer, 4, David E. Klutho, cover (top), 6, 14, 18, Heinz Kluetmeier, 13, John Biever, 26, 28, 30, John Iacono, cover (bottom), 5, 21, 25, 33, John W. McDonough, 16, 34, Peter Read Miller, 11, 20, 29, 32, 45 (bottom), Robert Beck, 8, 10, 15, 40, 42, 44 (top)

Design Elements: Shutterstock